BASIC KARATE

POCKET SPORTS BOOKS

BASIC KARATE

Edited by

IAIN MORRIS
(3rd Dan, Judo)

LONDON

W. FOULSHAM & CO. LTD.

NEW YORK   TORONTO   CAPE TOWN   SYDNEY

W. FOULSHAM & CO. LTD.
Yeovil Road, Slough, Bucks., England.

572-00585-7

MADE AND PRINTED IN GREAT BRITAIN BY
JOHN GARDNER (PRINTERS) LIMITED
HAWTHORNE ROAD, BOOTLE, LIVERPOOL, L20 6JX

CONTENTS

INTRODUCTION

The word *karate* itself literally means "empty hand" (kara—empty, te—hand). Although many of the earlier origins of the art are traced to China, it owes its development to the inhabitants of Okinawa in the Ryukya islands, some 200 miles to the southwest of Japan. At the beginning of the seventeenth century, the islands were conquered by the Japanese under the Daimyo of Satsuma. Like their Chinese predecessors, the Japanese would not allow the natives to carry weapons of any kind. But for their self-protection against their conquerers, the natives devised and elaborated the system of bare-hand fighting now known as *karate*. Then, as explained in the new edition of "The Fighting Spirit of Japan", it was the famous Okinawan karate master Funakoshi who later introduced it into Japan itself under the name of *karate-do*, or the "way" of karate. In this altered name we can see the analogy with judo, in which the word "do", meaning "way" was substituted by the late Dr. Jogoro Kano, the founder of judo, in order to emphasise the ethical basis of his new system of self-defence and physical culture.

Judo is called the "way of gentleness", whereas karate is often dubbed "the power way". But is the latter definition justified? Certainly in karate the full power of the body is employed when a blow is dealt, but this fact represents only one facet of the truth. It would be incomplete without taking account of the many occasions when small but well-trained *karateka* have defeated opponents vastly their superior in physical strength, and when karate veterans have easily disposed of powerful but inexperienced youngsters.

To close this introduction, I shall summarise the advantages officially claimed for karate: (1) Old people and children, men and women can practise it. (2) It can be practised amost anywhere without special equipment. (3) Given ordinary care, no danger is involved. (4) It can be practised singly or in company with others. Young and old men, both sexes without distinction, even those physically weak, may safely practise it without overtaxing themselves.

The *katas*, or forms, constitute the nucleus of karate practice; but they differ from the katas of judo or sumo in that the performer can regulate the degree of strength needed for their execution. The physically powerful performer can give an exhibition filled with force, while the weak performer can adapt his display to his individual capacity and execute the kata lightly. In this way the limitations of sex are taken into consideration and even when he or she suffers from certain physical disabilities, it is still possible to participate fully in karate practice. Then again, seeing that there are as many as thirty different katas in modern karate, the performer can choose those to his liking and freely execute a given number.

No special premises are required for the practice of karate. If a mat-covered floor is not available, an ordinary boarded floor will do as well. An open space, say in a garden or a courtyard, will suffice for the execution of the karate katas. On the other hand, regular *dojos* (exercise halls) are available in this country for the ever growing number of karate enthusiasts.

CHAPTER I

THE STRUCTURE OF KARATE—METHODS OF CLENCHING THE FIST—EMPI OR HIJIATE—HAND TECHNIQUES OR TEWAZA

In the language of the karate schools, the fist is called the "soul" of the art. Special attention must therefore be paid to the "*tempering*" or hardening of the fist in order to increase the efficacy of the blows dealt with it when held in various ways. Below are summarised the more important of these methods.

SEIKEN (*normal fist*). There are two methods, 1D and 3B. In *fig*. 1A the hand is shown with the thumb held outside, and the fingers close together. *Fig*. 1B The thumb has been slightly raised and all four finger-tips pressed into the palm.

Fig. 1 A

Fig. 1 B

Fig. 1C The thumb is held lower and the fingers bent and *fig:* 1D shows the thumb bent over the first finger and all four fingers pressed into the palm.

Fig. 1 C

Fig. 1 D

In *figs* 2 and 3B are demonstrated the two variations of the clenched fist; the first with the thumb bent over the forefinger and the second with the fore-finger extended and pressed into the palm. In this connexion, the Japanese author stresses the importance of keeping the fist tightly clenched at all times, otherwise there is a risk of injury when a blow is struck. The part used for attack with the *seiken* comprises the knuckles of the first and second fingers (*fig*. 3A)

Fig. 2

Fig. 3 A

Fig. 3 B

HIRAKEN (*flat or level fist*). In this method the four

fingers are shallowly clasped and the thumb presses against the side of the forefinger. The part used for attack is the second joint of the forefinger and middle finger (*fig.* 4). As a rule, the target is the opponent's face.

URAKEN (*back fist*). *Fig.* 5 shows how the fist is held. In this position the knuckle of the middle finger is generally used to attack the opponent's face.

KENTSUI (*hammer fist*). *Fig.* 6. In this position, the lower part of the edge of the palm is used in attack like a hammer. While beating off the opponent's wrist, the head of the fist and the hard part of the joints can also be used for attack.

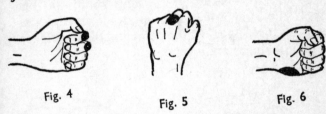

Fig. 4

Fig. 5

Fig. 6

HITOSASHIYUBI-IPPONKEN (*forefinger fist*). The fist is held in the *hiraken* position with the knuckle of the forefinger thrust forward (*fig.* 7). It is used to attack the opponent's solar-plexus (*suigetsu*) and the vital spot under the nose called *jinchu* in Japanese.

NAKAYUBI IPPONKEN (*middle finger fist*). With the fist held in the normal, *seiken*, the knuckle of the middle finger is projected (*fig.* 8). This method is used to attack the opponent's solar-plexus and *jinchu*.

Fig. 7

Fig. 8

TEGATANA (*piercing hand*). In this method the thumb is bent while the fingers are placed side-by-side and extended (*fig.* 9). The finger tips are used to thrust into the opponent's solar-plexus, and sides. Similarly, we have the Level Piercing Hand (*Hita-Nukite*) in which the back of the hand is turned upwards. *Fig.* 10 shows a two-finger Piercing Hand: In this method the ring finger, the little finger and the thumb are folded against the palm and the forefinger and middle finger are extended.

Fig. 9

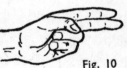

Fig. 10

This method is generally used to attack the opponent's eyes. The *One Finger* Piercing Hand (*fig.* 11) shows only the forefinger extended and is only used to attack the eyes.

TEGATANA (*handsword*). The thumb is bent and the four fingers extended. About two-thirds of the base of the palm are used in much the same way as the *kentsui* (*fig*. 12). The tegatana can be used to attack

Fig. 11

Fig. 12

the opponent's carotid arteries, his arms, temples, middle of the forehead and jinchu. In these cases you must be careful not to strike with the base of the little finger.

Base of the palm: The hand is held as in *fig*. 13 and is used to strike the opponent's face, chest and shoulders, with an upward thrusting movement. Similarly the thumb is folded into the palm and the shaded area in *fig*. 14 is used to strike upwards from under the opponent's jaw. The side of the thumb can also be used for the same purpose.

Fig. 13

Fig. 14

HIRA-HASAMI (*flat scissors*). The middle finger, ring

finger and little finger are slightly bent so that the thumb and forefinger form as it were a pair of scissors (*fig.* 15). The base of the thumb and forefinger are used to strike your opponent's neck muscles.

YUBI-HASAMI (*finger scissors*). The middle finger, ring finger and little finger are folded into the palm, leaving the thumb and forefinger in a position to thrust against your opponent's throat (*fig.* 16).

Fig. 15

Fig. 16

YUMI-KOBUSHI (*bow fist*). The thumb and the fingers are extended and held downwards with the wrist bent as in *fig.* 17. The shaded part of the illustration is chiefly used to parry blows.

KOTE (*forearm*). This is used to ward off an opponent's attack. For this purpose the forearm can be used in three ways. Firstly the outer forearm or *omotekote;* secondly, the reverse or rear forearm, *urakote;* thirdly the level forearm, *hirakote*, (*fig.* 18). These three divisions being marked a, b and c in *fig.* 18.

EMPI (*outstretched arm*) HIJIATE (*elbow*) *Attacks.* In karate, the elbow is used to attack the solar-plexus, chest and abdomen. With adequate training, **a** woman or even a child could make effective use of this natural weapon.

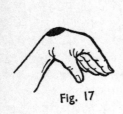

Fig. 17

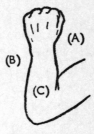

Fig. 18

TATE-EMPI (*vertical empi*). In this posture you stand with your fist touching your hip and your elbow held upwards. If both elbows are held upwards it becomes "both-vertical-empi" or *ryo-tate-empi.*

SAGETA EMPI (*lowered empi*). In this posture both elbows are held downwards in readiness for attack or for *hijiate.*

ZEN EMPI (*frontal empi*). This is one of the most frequently used methods of elbow attack or *hijiate.* The fist is brought up as far as the ear when the elbow is then driven back with maximum force into your opponent's solar-plexus. Used for instance when you are hugged from behind.

ZENGO EMPI (*front and rear empi*). When attacked by two opponent's, one from the front and one from the back, you use both elbows against the solar-plexus.

YOKO-EMPI (*lateral empi*). The right or left elbow is held horizontally in order to strike to either side, the fist being first brought in front of the chest. If both elbows are used the method is called "*ryo-yoko empi*".

HINERI-YOKO-EMPI (*twisting-lateral-empi*). Both fists are held with the thumbs against the breasts and the elbows opened. The shoulders must be kept lowered. In this posture the upper part of your body can be twisted to either side. And your left or right elbow is used simultaneously against the solar-plexus of an opponent attacking from the side or rear.

OTHER HAND TECHNIQUES OR TEWAZA

TSUKITE (*thrusting hand*). This, together with *ukete* is the most frequently used form of tewaza. The hand should be instantly withdrawn after the thrust to lessen the risk of it being countered, and also because a rebounding blow is more effective than a *dead* one.

UKETE (*defence hand*). This method is used as a defence against an opponent's hand or leg attack. It is classified into *jodan-uke*, *chudan-uke* and *gedan-uke*. For defences against the upper, middle and lower body respectively. Each *uke* is further divided into *uchi-uke* (inner-uke) and *soto-uke* (outer-uke). There are several variants, for example, there are the ude-uke in which the fist is half clenched, the tegatana-uke in which the fingers are stretched and the thumb bent for defence, the yoko-uke, etc.

HARAITE (*sweeping hand*). This is one kind of ukete in which you defend yourself by beating off an opponent's hand or leg attack. There are also subdivisions called uchi-barai (sweeping off), the tegatana-barai (handsword-sweep), etc.

YUMI-UKE (*bow-uke*). By means of the yumi-kobushi you ward off an opponent's thrusting hand from underneath.

KARETE (*hook-hand*). This is also a type of ukete whereby you intercept an opponent's hand thrust.

HIKITE (*pull-hand*). A variant of *karete*. As you parry your opponent's thrusting hand, you grasp it and pull it towards you. This enables you to disturb his balance and counter-attack more effectively.

HINERITE (*twisting hand*). A variant of *hikite*. Instead of simply pulling your opponent towards you, you twist him aside and counter-attack.

DAKITE (*hugging hand*). A kind of *ukete*. You grasp your opponent's thrusting hand, pull it towards and under your arm, then counter-attack.

SUKUITE (*scooping hand*). You scoop up your opponent's hand or leg and perhaps *throw* him; in any case his balance will be broken and you are in a good position to counter.

KAKIWAKE (*thrust aside*). If your opponent attacks with both hands, you dash them aside with your own wrists.

The foregoing methods may help to exemplify some of the more effective tewaza used to attack an opponent, or to nullify his own attacks against you.

CHAPTER II

WAYS OF PLANTING THE FEET
OR ASHI-NO-TACHI-KATA

MUSABITACHI (*linked feet*). The left and right heels are joined and the toes turned outwards (*fig*. 19A). The body is held upright without stiffness and the arms hang naturally at the sides. Your eyes are kept to the front.

Fig. 19 A   Fig. 19 B

HEISOKUTACHI (*blocked foot posture*). In this posture the feet are kept together from heel to toe (*fig*. 19B).

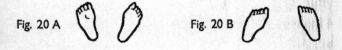

Fig. 20 A   Fig. 20 B

HACHIJITACHI (*figure eight posture*). The two forms of this posture, *soto-hachijitachi*, or outer figure eight posture, and *uchi-hachijitachi*, or inner figure eight posture, can be seen in *fig.* 20A and 20B respectively. The heels are usually separated by a distance roughly equal to the width of your shoulders.

Fig. 21 A   Fig. 21 B

REJITACHI. There are two positions, left and right, illustrated in *figs.* 21A and 21B.

TEIJITACHI (*T position*). The feet form a position which resembles an inverted letter T (*fig.* 21C.)

Fig. 21 C

ZENKUTSUTACHI (*inclined posture*). In this position the space between your feet will vary according to your height, but will generally be about 2 feet 5 inches. The advanced right leg is bent so that from knee to heel it is almost perpendicular. The rear leg is extended and the weight of the body is evenly distributed on both legs (*fig. 22*).

KOKUTSUTACHI (*rear inclined posture*). This is the reverse of the previous posture. Your rear left leg is bent to form a straight line from knee to heel and your right leg is extended forwards. The weight of your body is carried on the rear leg and the distance between the feet will be the same as in the previous posture (*fig. 23*).

Fig. 22

Fig. 23

NEKO-ASHITACHI (*cat foot posture*). Here your weight rests on your rear bent leg while your forward leg is also bent, but with the heel raised from the ground and the toes lightly applied (*fig. 24*). This posture is suitable for both advancing and retreating or *shintai* and for executing frontal kicks.

SAGI-ASHITACHI (*heron leg posture*). In this position one leg is lifted to the height of the other knee. If the lifted leg is in front of the knee it is called *mae-sagi-ashitachi*, or front heron leg posture (*fig.* 25), if behind, it becomes *ushiro-sagi-ashitachi*, or rear heron leg posture.

Fig. 24   Fig. 25

KIBATACHI (*horseman's posture*). The toes of both your feet are turned slightly inwards and the knees are bent so that from the knees to the heels the legs are almost perpendicular. You put your strength into the inner sides of the thighs and the outer edges of both feet. Your upper body is held upright with both shoulders lowered, the hips dropped and with a feeling of strength in the lower abdomen (*fig.* 26).

SHIKOTACHI (*four thigh posture*). In this posture your toes and knees are turned outwards as in the *soto-hachijitachi;* both legs are widely separated with

Fig. 26

Fig. 27

knees flexed, the upper body held upright and the hips lowered (*fig.* 27).

SANSENTACHI (*three battle posture*). Similar to the *kibatachi* but with either the left or right foot brought forward the distance from the toes to the heel (*fig.* 28).

FUDOTACHI (*Immobile posture*). In this posture your

legs are a little more widely separated than in the *zenkutsutachi*. Both knees are flexed and the weight

Fig. 28   Fig. 29

of the body is carried more or less equally on both legs (*fig.* 29).

CHAPTER III

LEG AND FOOT TECHNIQUES
OR ASHWAZA

The base of the toes at the bottom of a raised foot when the toes are curved back are likened to a pigeon's chest (*fig.* 30). They are the equivalent of the *seiken* (normal fist) and form the basis of *keriwaza* or kicking techiniques. When kicking in this way the ankle must be kept firm, otherwise there is a risk of injury.

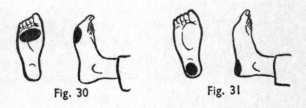

Fig. 30   Fig. 31

Part of the heel on the under surface of the foot can be used to stamp on your opponent's instep and to deliver the *keriage*, or upward kick, and the *kerihanashi* or kick release (*fig.* 31).

USHIROKAKATO (*back heel*) (*fig.* 32). This is used for

the *ushirogeri* or rear kick. When, for example, your waist is encircled from behind or your hand is twisted behind you, the rear kick can be effectively used against your opponent's shin or scrotum.

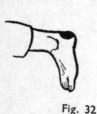

Fig. 32

Fig. 33

ASHIGATANA (*footsword*) (*fig.* 33) You curve the toes upwards and use the little toe edge of the foot for the *fumikomi*, or step-in, the kerihanashi or kick release, and *yokogeri* or lateral kick. Attacking your opponent's knees and sides. Care must be taken not to strike with the base of the little toe. The ashigatana corresponds to the tegatan of the hand techniques.

ASHIZOKO (*sole of the foot*). You use the sole of the foot to sweep away the opponent's attacking foot or hand. This method is not illustrated.

ASHIKUBI (*ankle*) (*fig.* 34). Your toes are stretched in a straight line with your shin in which position you attack your opponent's scrotum with the lower part of your ankle. This method can also be used to deliver the *maeqeri* or frontal kick to your opponent's solar-plexus or lower abdomen.

Fig. 34

HIZAGASHIRA (*knees*). Can be effectively used at close quarters or against an approaching opponent.

KERIHANASHI (*kick release*). Supporting your body on one leg, you kick with the other leg at your opponent's jaw, abdomen, shins or scrotum. The attacking leg must be instantly withdrawn to its original position so that your opponent has no chance to take advantage of you. The bottom of the foot is the part most used for kerihanashi.

KERIMKOMI (*kick-in*). Similar to kerihanashi, but instead of withdrawing the attacking foot you use it to sweep strongly against your opponent's knee-joint so as to dislocate it. If the foot is not used to kick but only to step in close, the method is called *fumokomi*.

KERIAGE (*upward kick*). Again similar to kerihanashi, but this time the sole of the foot or the top of the foot near the ankle is used.

YOKOGERI (*lateral kick*) (*fig.* 36). When attacked from the side, you can deliver kerihanashi with the edge of your foot. The method of kicking is to stand on either the right or left leg, then draw the other foot up to knee level (*fig.* 35) and strike powerfully sideways against your opponent's knee or chest in the kerihanashi style. Your foot is instantly withdrawn to its original position.

Fig. 35   Fig. 36

TOBIGERI (*jumping kick*). In this method you leap with both feet and kick your opponent's face or chest, with either your left or right foot. The object is to take him by surprise, or to get over a low defence. The kicking action must be performed very swiftly to avoid a possible counter-attack.

USHIROGERI (*rear kick*). If you are clasped from behind, you can bend your knees and kick backwards with the heel against your opponent's shin, etc.

KERIGAESHI (*return kick*). When countering your opponent's attacking arm or leg with kerihanashi, you simultaneously kick at him with the same leg. Also, when your kerihanashi is parried, you kick again without taking your leg back to its original position.

MAWASHI-GERI (*circular kick*). When attacked from either side, you turn and deliver a swinging kick behind your opponent's guard.

HIZATSUI (*knee hammer*). You strike upwards with your knee when at close quarters.

FUMIKIRI (*step out*). Using the ashigatana (edge of the foot), you kick at your opponent's leg with the sensation of stepping forward.

FUMITSUKI (*stamp down*). With the sole of your foot, you stamp on your opponent's instep and push him down.

FUMIUCHI (*step blow*). When grasped from behind, you stamp down on your opponent's instep with all your weight.

NAMIGAESHI (*wave counter*). With the sole of your foot, you beat off your opponent's attacking foot.

TOBIGOSHI (*jumping over*). In the case of a low level attack, a trained karateka may be able to jump right over his opponent, turn and kick.

YORIASHI (*approaching leg*). Attacking or retreating with short steps.

TOBIKOMIASHI (*jumping-in-leg*). When your opponent

is some distance away from you, you jump in and attack as soon as you see an opening.

NAGAESHI (*throwing leg*). This term applies to a technique designed to throw your opponent.

MIKKATSUKI ("*Three-day Moon*"). When your opponent advances towards you from the side to strike you with his fist, you seize his wrist from the inside, pull him towards you and simultaneously, kick at his chest with either leg.

SÁNKAKUTOBI (*triangle jump*). Assuming that you are attacked by three opponents, you take a running leap and kick the first; the second you strike with your head and the third with a left or right foot kick.

CHAPTER IV

TEMPERING THE HANDS AND FEET

In both the katas and *kumite* (karate contests), it is essential that you should not neglect the assiduous training of the natural weapons of your body. If you do, the power and efficacy of the art will be reduced by half. The most important items of auxiliary equipment are described below.

1. THE MAKIWARA. For the training and hardening of the hands and feet—the parts of the body used most often in attack and defence—the makiwara is the principal implement. The fixed type of makiwara consists of a post about seven feet long, of square timber, preferably cypress or cedar because of their elasticity. The width of the post is about four inches. The bottom two feet of the makiwara should be fixed in the ground, packed with bricks or other hard material to ensure stability, and the earth replaced and stamped firmly back into place. *Fig.* 37 gives a good idea of what the makiwara looks like when in position. The part of the post which is used for striking is bound with straw (*fig.* 38). The length of the straw rope used is about two feet and the thickness about three inches. Two of these straw bundles

C

are fixed to the makiwara, the upper one for hardening the hands and the lower for the feet. Suspended
sacks of sand or sawdust can also be used to harden
the hands and feet after preliminary toughening has
been carried out on the makiwara.

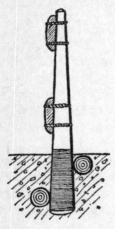

Fig. 37

Fig. 38

2. METHOD OF TRAINING THE SEIKEN (Normal Fist).
Take up your position at a convenient distance
facing the makiwara so that your outstretched hand
can touch the target without your having to lean
forward. Keep your upper body straight. The blow
with your right fist should coincide with a step forward on your left foot and the blow with your left
fist with a step forward on your right foot. Both
knees should be slightly bent and your hips should
be kept low. As *fig.* 39 shows, the back of the striking

fist, in this case the right, is held downward at the hip, and the back of the other fist upwards. You should practise striking the makiwara in all the postures already described in Chapter III.

Fig. 39

When striking with either fist, you must turn it so that the back of the fist is upwards just before impact; as you withdraw it, the fist should be turned again so that its back faces downwards by the time it reaches your hip. Whichever fist you strike with, the other is held at the hip with back downwards. It is essential to develop co-ordination between the striking fist and the withdrawing fist until the necessary degree of skill has been acquired. You should gradually increase the power of your blows; if you start too violently you may hurt your fists and be

forced to discontinue practice until they are better.
Once your fists have become throughly hardened,
you should be careful not to let them become soft
again. To achieve the maximum power in your blows,
the fist should be lightly closed at the start of the
movement and tightened only just before striking the

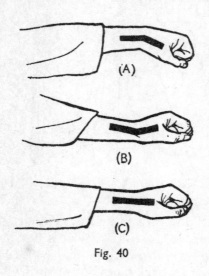

Fig. 40

makiwara. The speed of withdrawal is little greater
than that of the blow. On no account should your
wrist be bent, it must be held quite straight in order
to concentrate the full power of the blow and to
avoid personal injury. In the following illustrations,
fig. 40C is correct and the other two are incorrect
and potentially dangerous.

There are many other blows with the fist which can be practised on the makiwara, e.g., blows in an upward direction, sideways, jumping in from a distance to strike and many more from varying distances and angles. This sort of training is essential for the kumites, or free fighting, which you will come to at a later stage.

As a rule the arm is held so that the elbow is at right angles (*fig.* 41A). But it can also be held with the elbow drawn only half way back, to facilitate striking from close quarters (*fig.* 41B).

Fig. 41A   Fig. 41 B

The tempering of the seiken (normal fist) is carried out on both the stationary makiwara and on sand-bags. They serve to harden the fist, to develop speed of striking, to teach the right use of strength, to take up a position at the right distance from your opponent, to regulate your respiration, to cultivate strength in your arms, shoulders and abdomen, and to accustom the arm and shoulder joints to rapid reaction. Essentially there are four kinds of striking methods.

(i) CHOKUTSUKO *or direct thrust*. This is a fundamental method and is divided into three sections, i.e., the *Jodantsuki* or upper-level punch which is aimed at the opponent's face; the *Chudantsuki* or middle-level punch which is aimed at his chest, and the *Gedantsuki* or lower-level punch which is aimed at his abdominal region.

(ii) AGETSUKI *or rising punch*, otherwise the uppercut. In this method you ward off your opponent's attack, grip his attacking hand and pull him towards you. With your other hand clenched and moving upwards, you hit his jaw.

(iii) FURITSUKI *or swinging punch*. Swinging your fist to left or right you aim at your opponent's face or side.

(iv) WATSUKI *or circle punch*. When your striking fist is stopped by your opponent then from that position you describe a complete circle with it and deliver another blow.

3. AUXILIARY TRAINING

HIRAKEN (*flat or level fist*). Take up your position facing the mikiwara and train the fist by striking downward, slanting blows from above your head,

or direct blows from an oblique lateral position.
URAKEN (*under side fist*). Stand in a diagonal right or left lateral position and, bringing your right or left fist close to the opposite ear, strike the makiwara. Again, standing in front of the makiwara, turn the back of your fist from under the jaw towards the makiwara or from above your head (the back of the fist turned sideways) and strike from that position.

KENTSUI (*hammer fist*) From the same position as that in the previous example, you strike the makiwara with the sides of your fists.

NUKITE (*piercing hand*). When you are training the four-finger nukite on the makiwara, or sandbag, you must be careful to arrange the fingers correctly. Thrusting your extended fingers into boxes of sand or beans is part of the preliminary training, but if overdone, it can lead to deformed joints. Proceed with care and eventually your fingers will be tough enough to smash boards or damage an opponent's bones.

TEGATANA (*edge of the hand*). You hit the makiwara from the side standing diagonally in either left or right *kibatachi*. With the side of the hand palm downwards, commence from near the opposite ear.

TATE-EMPI *or vertical empi*. You stand sideways opposite the makiwara with your fist held in contact with your hip. From here the elbow is raised to strike. Imagine that you deal the blow upwards at the solar-plexus of an opponent approaching from the side.

SAGETA-EMPI *or lowered empi*. For this method a sandbag is placed on the ground and you drive your elbow downwards into it.

ZENEMPI *or frontal empi*. Stand in front of the maki-wara and bring your right or left fist up near your opposite ear. From this position you strike at the makiwara as though aiming at your opponent's chest or solar-plexus.

KOEMPI *or rear empi*. Stand with your back to the makiwara, one pace away from it. For high-level attacks (*jodantsuki*) your right or left fist starts from near the opposite ear; for middle-level attacks (*chudantsuki*), your fists start at the hip. In both cases the elbow must strike backwards into the makiwara with great speed and must then be instantly withdrawn to its original position.

YOKO-EMPI *or lateral empi*. As when training the tate-empi, you stand sideways before the makiwara, the back of your right or left fist turned downwards. After bringing your fist near your opposite shoulder you strike the makiwara with your elbow as though attacking an opponent's solar-plexus. The fist and elbow are horizontal in front of your chest at the moment of impact.

HINERI-YOKO-EMPI *or twisting-lateral-empi*. Stand in front of the makiwara with the thumb-edges of your right and left fists near your breasts, elbow extended. Taking a step forward, with your hips lowered, you strike with right then left elbows. At this moment you must be careful not to let the upper part of your body fall forward, and you must keep your shoulders firm.

UKETE (*defence hand*). Standing obliquely to the makiwara, you must strike with either hand, using the outer edge of the wrist, the thumb edge and the inside of the wrist according to the type of defence being performed. For example, when your attacking fist is parried by your opponent's forearm, the shock has to be absorbed by the inner, or pulse side of your wrist. Accordingly, this part must be toughened just as much as the striking edges of your wrists. When training the ukete, you should not bend the wrists but keep them firm and straight.

METHODS OF TEMPERING THE FEET: The training of the feet is particularly important in karate because of the extent to which they are used to attack and defend. The makiwara training must be performed in the various postures already described: fudotachi, nekoashitachi, zenkutsutachi etc. Facing the makiwara with the backs of your fists held against your hips, you kick with the rear foot in the case of fudotachi, and the front foot in nekoashitachi. After each kick the foot must be immediately brought back to its original position. The other striking parts of the foot are trained in the same way, though in the case of the ASHIGATANA or edge of the foot, you stand in a more sideways position to the makiwara.

CHAPTER V

FUNDAMENTAL TRAINING METHODS

The preliminary katas are divided into two main types, the *Renzoku-Renshuho* (successive training method) and the *Renketsu-Renshuho* (linking method). The former teaches the manner of advancing, retreating and moving sideways and the latter is designed to link all these methods. The Renzoku-Renshuho comprises the so-called *Shinko Kata* (advancing kata) in which we also find the *Chokusen Kata* (straight line kata) and the *Hasen Kata* (wave line kata). In *fig.* 42 the line marked "A" represents the straight line kata and the line marked "B" the wave line kata. The following is a description of the straight line kata:

1. CHUDANTSUKI (*middle level thrust*). These blows at your opponent's middle body are the most important of the fundamental ones and must be practised continually until mastered.

Principle: Chudan-Renzoku-Oitsuki (middle-level-successive-pursuit-thrust). At the word of command you assume the outer hachijitachi posture and then the left zenkutsutachi posture as illustrated in *figs.* 43 and 44. Your right hand is held

obliquely towards the left side with the palm open
and turned upwards. Your left hand is held in front
of your left shoulder with the palm upwards. Then,
you withdraw your right hand, closing it as you do
so, until the fist is strongly clenched and resting

Fig. 42   Fig. 43   Fig. 44

against your right hip. At the same time, your left
hand is clenched and lowered until it is six or seven
inches above your left knee, with the outer edge of
your wrist held in the gedan-uke position ready to
defend against any low level attack. Your hips are
lowered and your upper body is upright and turned
to the right. Your feet face ahead and you should
have a feeling of strength in your lower abdomen.

The face is turned to the front, your eyes fixed on an imaginary opponent.

At the command "*Hajime!*" (begin) you assume the posture shown in *fig*. 45 with your right foot planted a good pace in front of your left in the right

Fig. 45

senkutsutachi position. Your left fist is held firmly against your left hip in readiness to grasp an opponent's attacking hand or leg and pull it towards you. Your right fist is extended with the back upwards, preparatory to thrusting at the solar-plexus of an opponent standing in front of you. Your advanced foot should be allowed to slide forward without any weight being put on it and without lifting it off the ground.

The advanced foot is planted on the ground just before you strike with your right fist, not at the same time. On the other hand, the blow with the right fist must be accompanied by a simultaneous withdrawal of the left fist to your hip. If the thrust and with-drawal are made simultaneously, then even if your first attack has failed you are in a position to defend against a counter-attack. The posture at the time of the blow is with the shoulders lowered and firm, the wrist held with the top of the fist being in a straight line from the shoulder and the upper part of the body facing the opponent. Practise this movement alternatively left and right.

In the case of the *Chudan-Renzoku-Gyakutsuki*, you assume the outer hachijitachi posture at the word of command, and then, as for the previous method (*oitsuki*), the left zenkitsutachi posture in preparation for the gedan-uke (lower level defence). After first standing with your right fist in contact with your right hip, as shown in *fig*. 46. you raise your right fist for the chedantsuki or middle level blow when your left fist is brought against your left hip. This is the preparatory posture. When the command "*Hajime*" is given, you take a step forward with your right foot, your left fist is raised for the chudantsuki and your right fist is brought to your right hip.

This action, of the striking fist being accompanied by a step forward with the opposite foot, gives this method its name, i.e., "*gyakutsuki*", or reverse blow.

In this way you also train in the kibatachi, and shikotachi, and for the jodan, chudan and gedan attacks. Practise alternatively with the left and right hand as many as a hundred or two hundred times to develop staying power.

Fig. 46

2. JODANTSUKI. In this style you attack your opponent's face. The principle is identical with that of the chudantsuki.

3. GEDANTSUKI. In this style your attack is directed against your opponent's abdominal region (gedan = middle level). Or when your opponent tries to kick you, you thrust his leg down with your hand.

4. WAY OF TURNING RIGHT OR LEFT. If, when executing jodantsuki, chudantsuki, or gedantsuki and

striking alternatively left and right, you find that your advance is blocked, you utter a shout (kiai shout) and move round to either side to deal another blow. In the case of oitsuki, for example, when you are standing in the left zenkutsutachi posture you turn 180 degrees on the left heel as an axis and finish facing the opposite way in the right zenkutsutachi position. Your right fist is held in gedanuke style about six or seven inches above the knee, and your left fist is at your left hip. While turning, you adopt the gedan-uke posture as though to ward off a kick from the rear. You then advance in the manner already described. The same principle is used when turning to the left and when turning from the gyakutsuki to left or right.

5. GEDAN-UKE (*lower level defence*). From the outer hachijitachi posture you take a step to the rear and assume the left zenkutsutachi posture. With your left fist you execute the gedan-uke and bring your right fist to your right hip. While executing the gedan-uke left and right you advance as far as you are able and then, in the last defensive position, you utter the kiai shout and retreat.

6. CHUDAN-TEGATANA-UKE (*middle level defence*). When your opponent attacks the area of your chest, you defend yourself by means of a blow with the edge of your hand.

Principle: In preparation for the chudan-renzoko-tegatana-uke you adopt the outer hachijitachi posture and from that position you withdraw your right

foot to the rear to take up the nekoashitachi posture.
With your right hand forming a tegatana in front of
your chest, your left hand forms a tegatana starting
from the front of your right shoulder, back of the
hand downwards with the elbows half bent, you face
your imaginary opponent and deal a sweeping blow
at the middle of his body (*fig.* 47). When your left

Fig. 47   Fig. 48

hand is withdrawn to your right shoulder the back of
the hand is turned downwards, but just before the
blow is struck at the opponent's hand or foot, the
hand is turned so that the back faces obliquely
upwards. The finger tips of the tegatana are generally
held at the height of the shoulder.

At the command of "*Hajime*", you step forward with your right foot in front of your left and adopt the nekoashitachi posture. At the same time you make a left tegatana in front of your chest and a right tegatana in the chudan-uke style, repeating this action alternately right and left as you advance.

7. JODAN-AGE-UKE (*upper level rising defence*). When your opponent aims a blow at your upper body, you defend yourself by sweeping his attacking hand upwards from below.

Principle: From the outer hachijitachi posture, at the word of command for the jodan-renzoku-age-uke preparatory posture (*fig. 48*), your right foot is withdrawn a pace so that you adopt the left fudotachi posture. At the same time, your right fist is brought to your right hip and the back of your left fist is turned inwards, with the little finger edge upwards. and sweeps up above your forehead.

At the start you step forward with your right foot and adopt the right fudotachi posture. At the same time you withdraw your left fist to your left hip, and sweep upwards above your forehead. When executing the jodan-uke, you ward off from below, the opponent's attacking hand with the underside of your forearm. As you advance, you practise the jodan-age-uke alternately left and right, keeping your upper body straight and firm.

8. JODAN-UCHI-KOMI (*upper level drive-in*). You attack your imaginary opponent's face or shoulder area with the side of your fist (*kentsui*) or, assuming

D

that your opponent strikes at your upper body, you reply with a kentsui and beat down his attacking hand.

Principle: At the word of command for preparation for the jodan-renzoku-ychi-komi (*upper-level-successive-drive-in*), from the outer hachijitachi posture (*fig.* 49) you draw your right foot back a

Fig. 49   Fig. 50

step and adopt a right kokutsutachi posture with your right fist against your right hip. Your left fist is held above your head, little finger edge upwards, and you immediately deal a blow in a diagonally downward direction. At the moment of the blow the back of the left fist is turned obliquely downwards.

At the command of *"Hajime"*, you step forward a pace with your right foot in front of your left to assume the left kokutsutachi posture. Your left fist is at your left hip and with your right fist you execute the jodan-uchi-komi blow. Repeat these movements left and right as you advance, and when you cannot advance at the moment of the last uchi-komi you utter the kiai shout and withdraw.

9. KERI-KOMI (*kick-in*). This method has already been described in the section on ashwaza, or foot and leg techniques, but a paragraph on the method of training for the *renzoku-keri-komi*, or successive kick-in will not go amiss. At the word of command to get ready you adopt the outer hachijitachi posture, and then pass to the left zenkutsutachi posture (*fig.* 50) with both fists against your hips, the backs of the hands turned downwards.

At the word of command to begin, you kick to the front with the sole of your right foot (*fig.* 51) and then instantly withdraw the foot to its original position when the thigh and shin are perpendicular. You step forward as shown in *fig.* 52.

When you kick with your right foot, the knee of your left leg being slightly bent, your fists remain at your hips at all times and you will kick as strongly and as high as possible. In an actual fight, however, you should take care not to kick too high, otherwise your opponent would be able to take advantage of the resulting loss of balance. As you advance you kick alternately left and right. Right turn: When

turning to the right you continue to keep your fists
on your hips, then advance in the new direction as
before.

10. YOKO-GERI (*lateral kick*). This method can be
performed with the edge of the foot or with the sole.
The explanation given below refers to the method
using the edge of the foot.

Fig. 51

Fig. 52

Principle: At the word of command to get ready
for the renzoku ashigatana, or successive kick with
the edge of the foot, you adopt the outer hachijitachi
posture in a right lateral kicking direction. Both
hands are closed in the seiken style and rest on the
hips with the backs turned downwards, or the palms
of the hands can rest on the hips with the thumbs
against the forefingers.

At the word of command to begin you stand as shown in *fig.* 53 with your left leg passed a step in front of your right. As shown in *fig.* 54 your right foot is then raised and you kick with the edge of the foot directly sideways at your imaginary opponent's sides or abdomen.

Fig. 53   Fig. 54

The foot is then withdrawn and slightly lowered and you take up the outer hachijitachi posture. Concurrently for the second time, after advancing your left foot a pace sideways across your right leg, you kick to the side with an ashigatana.

When kicking, you must not bend your upper body but keep it quite upright. For the lateral kick you do not make a right or left turn, i.e. while kicking with a right ashigatana you advance sideways and when your advance is forced to a stop, retaining that posture, you begin again in the opposite direction. You take a step to the side with your right foot in front of your left foot and deliver a left lateral ashigatana kick. Practise these movements repeatedly as you advance sideways.

There are many more successive training methods than those already described, but at this stage the above will suffice. All these methods are designed to cultivate standing posture, and staying power; it is of great importance to practise all these movements until they can be performed with speed and assurance. Moreover, not only must you practise the movements in a straight line for advance and retreat but also in the wave-like or undulating line. If you master the straight line then you ought naturally to be able to understand the principle of the wave-like kata.

In what is called the *renketsu renshuho* (linking training), you combine movements. For example, at the same time as you make the chudantsuki, or middle-level blow, you can advance with your fist ready for a gedanbarai or low-level sweep, starting off alternately from the left and right foot. And when doing the jodan-age-uke or upper-level rising defence in order to deliver a gedan-tegatana-barai or low-level sweep with the edge of the hand, changing the postures while advancing and retreating, you combine the two foregoing methods of training with the left and right leg alternately.

CHAPTER VI

KARATE KATA

Seeing that in karate, unlike judo, very few methods can be demonstrated to their logical conclusion without the risk of seriously injuring an opponent, you must halt any movement a split second before reaching the target. Special importance is naturally ascribed to the study and practice of the karate katas, or formal demonstrations.

In this section I have confined myself to a description of the most important karate kata, viz., the Dai Nihon Karate-do Ten-no-Data (Great Japan Karate-way Heavenly Kata) devised by the celebrated karate teacher *Funakoshi*.

In the performance of these katas a very strict etiquette is observed. In Japan, it is customary when a formal demonstration is being given for the performer or performers to salute standing, first the shrine of the *kami* or god and then the *shihan* or master presiding on the occasion. The method of salutation is shown in *fig.* 55.

OMOTE-NO-1. *Chudan-oitsuki* (middle level pursuit blow)

Preparation: From the heisokutachi posture you

take up the outer hachijitachi posture, your feet about one foot five inches apart, your shoulders lowered and your fists resting lightly on your thighs. Strength should be infused into your lower abdomen while your gaze is fixed on your imaginary opponent in front of you (*figs.* 56A and 56B.)

Fig. 55   Fig. 56 A   Fig. 56 B

(1) Take a big step forward with your right foot and assume the right zenkutsutachi posture while with your right fist you deal a blow at the middle of your opponent's body, then simultaneously withdraw your left fist to your left hip (*fig.* 57).

The instant your right fist has reached its imaginary target you utter the kiai shout. Your posture at the time of striking is with your upper body slightly

inclined forward but your right shoulder must not
be pushed forward. Your body weight is carried
equally on both legs and care must be taken not to
put too much strength into your right foot when
stepping forward. The right foot must not be raised
from the floor but slid along it.

Fig. 57

(2) Withdraw your right foot to its former position
lowering both fists and revert to the preparatory
posture.

(3) Movement is the reverse of (1). And (4) is the
reverse of (2).

OMOTE-NO-2. *Jodan-oitsuki* (upper-level pursuit
blow)

(1) From the preparatory posture you take a big step forward and assume the right zenkutsutachi posture.

At the same time, while you withdraw your left fist to your left hip, you strike at the face of your imaginary opponent with your right fist (*fig.* 58), and utter the kiai shout. While striking, you must take care not to let your fist swerve off target or to let your shoulder move forward.

Fig. 58   Fig. 59

(2) Withdraw your right foot to its former position lowering both fists and revert to the preparatory posture.

(3) Movement is the reverse of (1). And (4) the reverse of (2).

OMOTE-NO-3. *Chudan-takutsuki* (middle-level reverse blow)

(1) You start from the preparatory posture with a forward step of your left foot to assume the left fudotachi posture. Having brought your right fist to your right hip, while your left fist is at your left hip you raise your right fist and strike forward with a chudantsuki or middle level blow (*fig.* 59).

At the instant of the blow you utter the kiai shout. An important point in connection with the fudotachi posture is that when you step forward with the left foot, although your lower body must naturally be turned diagonally right, your upper body must face forward with the shoulders kept low.

(2) Your left foot is withdrawn, both your fists are lowered and you revert to the preparatory posture.

(3) Movement is the reverse of (1). And (4) the reverse of (2).

OMOTE-NO-4. *Jodan-gyakutsuki* (upper level reverse blow)

(1) With your left foot you take a big pace forward and assume the left fudotachi posture. Having placed your right fist at your right hip and while your left fist is withdrawn to your left hip you raise your right fist and strike upwards at your imaginary opponent's body (*fig.* 60), uttering the kiai shout the moment your fist reaches its supposed target.

(2) As you bring your left foot to its former position you lower both fists and revert to the preparatory posture.

(3) Movement is the reverse of (1). And (4) is the reverse of (2).

OMOTE-NO-5. *Gedanbarai-chudantsuki* (lower level sweep-middle level blow)

(1) You take a step backwards with your right foot to assume the left fudotachi posture. Your right fist is held at your right hip. Starting from your right

Fig. 60

shoulder with the back of the hand downwards, you strike a blow with your left fist diagonally downwards to about six inches above your left knee.

As you strike, the left fist is turned so that the back of the hand faces upwards at the end of the action. The striking area is the back of the left forearm, (*fig.* 61).

(2) While your left fist is withdrawn to your left hip your right fist delivers a middle level blow. Your feet do not move and you utter the kiai at the moment the blow reaches its target.

Fig. 61

(3) Your right foot is brought slowly back to its former position, your fists are lowered and you revert to the preparatory posture.

(4) Movement is the reverse of (1), (5) the reverse of (2), and (6) the reverse of (3).

When practising these movements you should aim at performing the defensive and attacking actions at the same time.

OMOTE-NO-6. *Chudan-ude-uke-chudantsuki* (Middle level arm defence—middle level blow).

(1) From the preparatory posture you take a step to

the rear with your right foot and assume the left
fudotachi posture. Your right fist is held against your
right hip. With your left fist starting from the right
shoulder, the back turned upwards, the elbow half
bent and serving as the centre you describe an arc
and deal a sweeping blow at the middle of your
imaginary opponent's body (*fig.* 62). The sweep-

Fig. 62

ing blow is dealt with the thumb-edge of your wrist
at the opponent's chest area. The fist is held at
shoulder height with the back turned downwards.
(2) Your feet in the same position, your left fist is
drawn to your left hip and you deliver a middle level
blow with your right fist, uttering the kiai as you do
so.

(3) You slowly withdraw your feet to their former position, lower both fists and resume the preparatory posture.

(4) Movement is the reverse of (1), (5) the reverse of (2), and (6) the reverse of (3).

OMOTE-NO-7. *Chudan-tegatana-uke-chudan-nukite* (middle level defence with the edge of the hand—middle level finger-tip thrust).

(1) Withdrawing your right foot a pace to the rear you assume the right kokutsutachi posture. Your right fist is held against your right hip. Preparatory to a tegatana your left hand starts from your right shoulder, the back turned downwards, the elbow half bent and the blow is dealt with a sweeping action when the back of the hand is turned obliquely upwards (*fig.* 63).

(2) Here you stand with your legs in much the same position. But in this case your left fist is held at your left hip while your right hand is opened to deal a thrust with the finger-tips at the frontal middle area of an imaginary opponent (*fig* 64). At the instant of the blow you utter the kiai. Your shoulders should not be raised when delivering the thrust and you should have a feeling of strength in the armpits.

(3) Your right leg is brought back to its former position. Both your hands are lowered and you revert to the preparatory posture.

(4) Movement is the reverse of (1), (5) the reverse of (2), and (6) the reverse of (3).

OMOTE-NO-8. *Jodan-tegatanabarai-jodantsuki* (upper

level sweep with the edge of the hand—upper level blow)

(1) From the preparatory posture you withdraw your right foot a pace to the rear to assume the left fudotachi posture. Your right fist is held against your right hip and your left arm is raised in preparation for a tegatana, the elbow half bent. With

Fig. 63

Fig. 64

the elbow as centre you describe an arc as though to ward off an attack and strike a sweeping blow at eye level, finishing with the palm turned to the front (*fig.* 65).

(2) With your feet in the same position and your left fist held at your left hip, you strike at the upper part

(jodan) of your imaginary opponent, uttering the kiai at the same time. When you have warded off your opponent's attack with a left tegatana, you seize his wrist, pull him towards your left hip and once his posture has been broken, strike at his upper body with your right fist.

Fig. 65

(3) You bring your right foot back to its former position, lower both fists and resume the preparatory posture.

(4) Movement is the reverse of (1), (5) the reverse of (2), and (6) the reverse of (3).

OMOTE-NO-9. *Jodan-uke-chudantsuki* (upper level rising defence—middle level blow)

E

(1) You withdraw your right foot a pace to the rear and take up the left fudotachi posture. Your right fist is held at your right hip and your left fist is raised above your forehead with the back of the hand turned inwards, the little finger uppermost as you sweep the fist upwards (*fig.* 66). The defence against an

Fig. 66

upper level attack is performed with an upward-springing action of the hands, but not the wrist and forearm alone. You must lower your hips and defend with your whole body. The reason for this is that if you defend yourself with only your wrist and you are facing an opponent as strong or stronger than you are, you may fail to complete your defence.

At the time of the defence the distance between the back of your fist and your forehead is about five or six inches. Your elbows are raised to protect your sides, and your upper body is tilted slightly forward. (2) Your feet are in the same position. Your left fist is at your left hip and with your right fist, you strike at the middle (chudan) of your imaginary opponent and utter the kiai.

Fig. 67

(3) You bring your right foot back, lower both fists and resume the preparatory posture.
(4) Movement is the reverse of (1), (5) is the reverse of (2), and (6) is the reverse of (3).
OMOTE-NO-10. *Jodan-uchikomi-chudantsuki* (upper level strike-in—middle level blow).

(1) You withdraw your right foot a pace to the rear and assume the left fudotachi posture with your right fist at your right hip and your left fist raised, the little finger edge upwards in front of your eyes (*fig.* 67). From this position you strike obliquely downwards. The distance of your left fist from your eyes is about sixteen inches. The imaginary opponent may resist the upper level attack by striking it aside with the kentsui (side of the fist) or with the wrist. You may then strike his face, etc., with your own kentsui.

(2) With your feet in the same position and your left fist at your left hip, you strike at the opponent's middle body with your right fist, uttering the kiai.

(3) You bring your feet back to their former position, lower both fists and resume the preparatory posture.

(4) Movement is the reverse of (1), (5) the reverse of (2), and (6) the reverse of (3).

CHAPTER VII

KATA OF KUMITE

In karate, when kata is being performed by two partners, the attacker is called *Semete* and the defender *Ukete*. As already explained in these pages the karate name for contest is kumite. The first type of kumite I shall try to describe is often called *yakusoku kate*, or "agreement kata", because it is essential for the safety of both partners that it should be demonstrated in a strictly pre-arranged sequence of movements.

URA-NO-1. *Gedanbarai-chudantsuki* (lower level sweep—middle level blow)

As in the other katas, Semete and Ukete salute the presiding Master and then each other, standing about three feet apart in the outer hachijitachi posture (*fig.* 68).

At the word of command to prepare, Semete (on the left) withdraws his right foot a pace, assumes the left zenkutsutachi posture and poises his left fist for a sweeping lower level blow. His right fist is at his right hip and he gazes straight at his opponent's eyes.

Ukete stands in the outer hachijitachi posture and

Fig. 68

Fig. 69

also watches his opponent's eyes. It is essential that both performers should preserve an unmoved mental attitude in both attack and defence (*fig.* 69).

(1) At the word of command, Semete utters the kiai, steps forward a pace with his right foot and assuming the right zenkutsutachi posture, strikes a blow at Ukete's lower body, at the same time bringing his left fist to his left hip.

Fig. 70

Ukete withdraws his right foot a pace to the rear, assumes the left zenkutsutachi posture and sweeps the attacking wrist from the inside with his left fist, bringing his right fist to his right hip (*fig.* 70).

(2) At the word of command Semete assumes the posture for a lower level blow.

Ukete brings his left fist to his left hip and uttering the kiai, aims a blow at Ukete's chest with his right fist (*fig.* 71).

(3) At the word of command Semete withdraws his right foot to the preparatory posture.

Fig. 71

Ukete advances his right foot to the preparatory posture. At the preparatory word of command Semete steps back a pace with his left foot, assuming the right zenkutsutachi posture, and as he prepares his right fist for the sweeping lower level blow, he places his left fist against his left hip.

Ukete also assumes the preparatory posture, in this case the opposite foot and hand position to *fig.* 69.

(1) At the word of command Semete steps forward a pace with his left foot and, assuming the left zenkutsutachi posture, utters the kiai and aims a blow with his left fist at Ukete's lower body, bringing his right fist to his right hip.

Fig. 72

Ukete withdraws his left foot and assumes the right zenkutsutachi posture as he defends himself with his right fist in a sweeping lower level style, bringing his left fist to his left hip (*fig.* 72).

(2) At the word of command Semete assumes the same posture.

Ukete places his right fist against his hip, utters the kiai and delivers a middle level blow with his left fist.

(3) At the word of command Semete withdraws his left foot to the preparatory posture.

Ukete advances his left foot to the preparatory posture. The movements are each executed twice, then after the first demonstration Semete and Ukete exchange roles and practise them again twice each. The same rule applies to the rest of the kata.

URA-NO-2. *Chudan-ude-uke-chudantsuki* (middle level arm defence—middle level blow)

At the preparatory word of command Semete, from the outer hachijitachi posture takes a pace to the rear with his right foot and assumes the left zenkutsutachi posture. His left fist is poised for a sweeping lower level blow and his right fist is at his right hip.

Ukete stands in the same preparatory posture.

(1) At the word of command Semete steps forward a pace with his right foot and, assuming the right zenkutsutachi posture with his left fist at his left hip, utters the kiai and strikes a middle level blow with his right fist (*fig.* 73).

Ukete withdraws his right foot a pace and assumes the left fudotachi posture with his right fist at his right hip. At the same time he wards off Semete's attack with a sweeping blow outwards with his left fist (thumb edge), as shown in *fig.* 74.

(2) At the word of command Semete assumes the same posture.

Ukete with his left fist at his left hip utters the kiai

Fig. 73

Fig. 74

and aims a middle level blow with his right fis
(*fig.* 75).

(3) At the word of command Semete takes a step to
the rear with his right foot and assumes the pre
paratory posture.

Fig. 75

Ukete advances a pace with his right foot and
assumes the preparatory posture.

At the preparatory word of command Semete
withdraws his left foot a pace to the rear and, assuming the right zenkutsutachi posture, prepares for a
sweeping lower level blow with his right fist, holding
his left fist at his left hip.

Ukete is in the preparatory posture.

1) At the word of command Semete steps forward a pace with his left foot and assumes the left zen-kutsutachi posture with his right fist at his right hip. Then uttering the kiai he aims a middle level blow with his left fist.

Fig. 76

Ukete withdraws his left foot a pace to the rear and, assuming the right fudotachi posture, sweeps Semete's attacking arm to the side with his right wrist, holding his left fist against his left hip (*fig.* 76).
(2) At the word of command Semete is in the same posture. Ukete, his right fist held at his right hip, utters the kiai and delivers a middle level blow with his left fist (*fig.* 77).

(3) At the word of command Semete withdraws his left foot a pace and assumes the preparatory posture.

Ukete advances his left foot a pace and also assumes the preparatory posture. Afterwards Semete and Ukete exchange roles and repeat the practice.

Fig. 77

URA-NO-3. *Chudan-tegatana-uke-chudan-nukite* (middle level edge-of-the-hand defence—middle level finger-tip thrust).

At the preparatory word of command Semete from the outer hachijitachi posture withdraws his right foot a pace to the rear and assumes the left zenkutsutachi posture. His left fist is poised for a

sweeping lower level blow and his right fist is at his
right hip.

Ukete is also in the preparatory posture.

(1) At the word of command Semete takes a step to
the front with his right foot and assumes the right
zenkutsutachi posture with his left fist at his left hip.
At the same time he utters the kiai and aims a middle
level blow with his right fist.

Fig. 78

Ukete withdraws his right foot a pace to the rear,
assumes the right kokutsutachi posture and with a
left tegatana slanting outwards, sweeps aside his
opponent's right wrist (*fig.* 78).

(2) At the word of command Semete assumes the
same posture.

Ukete relaxes his left tegatana, clenches his fingers and brings the hand to his left hip. At the same time opening his right fist he thrusts at his opponent's middle body with the finger-tips (nukite) (*fig.* 79).
(3) At the word of command Semete steps back a pace with his left foot and assumes the right zenkutsutachi posture with his left fist at his left hip and his right fist ready to deliver a sweeping lower level body blow.

Fig. 79

Ukete is in the preparatory posture.
(1) At the word of command Semete advances his left foot a pace and, assuming the left zenkutsutachi posture with his right fist at his right hip, utters the kiai and strikes at Ukete's middle body.

Ukete withdraws his left foot a pace to the rear and assumes the right kokutsutachi posture with his left fist at his left hip. His right hand is opened in a tegatana and he sweeps away his opponent's left wrist from the inside (*fig.* 80).

Fig. 80

(2) At the word of command Semete assumes the same posture.

Ukete, with his right fist at his right hip and his left hand opened, aims a thrust with the finger tips at his opponent's middle body uttering the kiai at the same time.

(3) At the word of command Semete retracts his left foot and assumes the preparatory posture.

Ukete advances his left foot and also assumes the

F

preparatory posture. Semete and Ukete then exchange roles and repeat the practice.

URA-NO-4. *Jodan-tegatana-harai-jodantsuki* (upper level: edge-of-the-hand sweep)

(1) At the preparatory word of command Semete steps back a pace with his right foot and assumes the left zenkutsutachi posture. At the same time he holds his right fist at his right hip and his left fist in the lower level sweeping position.

Fig. 81

Ukete stands in the preparatory posture.

Semete takes a big step forward with his right foot and, assuming the right zenkutsutachi posture with his left fist at his left hip, utters the kiai and strikes at his opponent's upper body with his right fist (*fig.*81).

Ukete withdraws his right foot and, assuming the left fudotachi posture with his right fist at his right hip, wards off his opponent's attack (*fig.* 82).

Fig. 82

(2) At the word of command Semete assumes the same posture. With his left hand Ukete grasps his opponent's right wrist and with a twisting action draws it towards himself. Then to the accompaniment of the kiai he strikes at his opponent's face or upper body with his right fist (*fig.* 83).

(3) At the word of command Semete withdraws his right foot to the preparatory posture.

Ukete advances his right foot, relinquishes his left-hand grip on Semete's right wrist and assumes the preparatory posture.

At the preparatory word of command Semete, from the preparatory posture, steps a pace to the rear with his left foot and assumes the right zenkutsutachi posture with his left hand at his left hip and his right fist in the lower level sweeping position.

Ukete stands in the preparatory posture.

Fig. 83

(1) At the word of command Semete advances a pace with his left foot and assumes the left zenkutsutachi posture with his right fist at his right hip. Then uttering the kiai he aims a blow at his opponent's face with his left fist. Ukete withdraws his left foot a pace and, assuming the right fudotachi posture with his left fist at his left hip, wards off his opponent's left wrist with a right tegatana (*fig.* 84).

Fig. 84

Fig. 85

(2) At the word of command Semete assumes the same posture.

Ukete grasps his opponent's left wrist with his right hand and draws it towards himself with a twisting action; then uttering the kiai he strikes at his opponent's upper body with his left fist (*fig.* 85).

(3) At the word of command Semete withdraws his left foot and assumes the preparatory posture.

Ukete withdraws his left foot, lets go his hold on his opponent's left wrist and assumes the preparatory posture.

Semete and Ukete then exchange roles and repeat the movement twice.

URA-NO-5. *Jodan-age-uke-chudantsuki* (upper level lifting defence—middle level blow)

At the preparatory word of command Semete takes a step back with his right foot and, assuming the left zenkutsutachi posture with his right fist at his right hip, prepares his left fist for a lower level sweeping blow.

Ukete is in the preparatory posture.

(1) At the word of command Semete steps forward with his right foot and, assuming the right zenkutsutachi posture with his left fist at his left hip, utters the kiai and aims a blow at Ukete's upper body with his right fist.

Ukete draws his right foot back a pace and assumes the left fudotachi posture, his right fist at his right hip. Then with the wrist of his left hand he knocks his opponent's right fist upwards (*fig.*86).

Fig. 86

Fig. 87

(2) At the word of command Semete assumes the same posture.

Ukete, his left fist at his left hip, utters the kiai and delivers a blow at Semete's middle body with his right fist (*fig.* 87).

(3) At the word of command Semete withdraws his right foot to the preparatory posture.

Ukete advances his right foot and assumes the preparatory posture. At the preparatory word of command Semete withdraws his left foot a pace and assumes the right zenkutsutachi posture, his left fist at his left hip and his right fist ready for a sweeping lower level blow.

Ukete is in the preparatory posture.

Fig. 88

(1) At the word of command Semete advances his left foot a pace and assumes the left zenkutsutachi posture, his right fist at his right hip. Then uttering the kiai he strikes at Ukete's upper body with his left fist.

Fig. 89

Ukete steps back a pace and assumes the right fudotachi posture, his left fist at his left hip, and with the wrist of his right fist he knocks his opponent's left hand upwards (*fig.* 88).

(2) At the word of command Semete assumes the same posture.

Ukete with his right fist at his right hip utters the kiai and strikes at Semete's middle body with his left fist (*fig.* 89).

(3) At the word of command Semete withdraws his left foot to the preparatory posture.

Ukete steps forward with his left foot and resumes the preparatory posture. At the close of these movements Semete and Ukete exchange roles as before and repeat the practice twice.

URA-NO-6. *Jodan-uckikomi-chudantsuki* (upper level strike-in—middle level blow)

At the preparatory word of command Semete from the outer hachijitachi posture draws his right foot back a pace and assumes the left zenkutsutachi posture, his right fist at his right hip and his left fist poised for a sweeping lower level blow.

Ukete is in the preparatory posture.

(1) At the word of command Semete advances a pace with his right foot and assumes the right zenkutsutachi posture, his left fist at his left hip. Then uttering the kiai he strikes at Ukete's upper body with his right fist.

Ukete steps back with his right foot and assumes the left fudotachi posture, his right hand at his right hip. Then raising his left hand high he strikes down his opponent's wrist with the side of his fist or with his own wrist obliquely from above (*fig.* 90).

(2) At the word of command Semete resumes his posture.

Ukete with his left fist at his left hip, utters the kiai and strikes at his opponent's middle body with his right fist (*fig.* 91).

(3) At the word of command Semete retracts his right foot and assumes the preparatory posture.

Ukete advances his right foot and resumes the

Fig. 90

Fig. 91

preparatory posture. At the preparatory word of command Semete withdraws his left foot and assumes the right zenkutsutachi posture, his left fist at his left hip, and at the same time poises his right fist for a sweeping lower level blow.

Ukete is in the preparatory posture.

(1) At the word of command Semete steps forward and, assuming the left zenkutsutachi posture with his right fist at his right hip, he utters the kiai and strikes Ukete's upper body with his left fist.

Fig. 92

Ukete takes a pace backwards and assumes the right fudotachi posture. Then, raising his right fist high, he brings the side of his fist or his wrist down against his opponent's attacking hand in a slanting direction (*fig.* 93).

2) At the word of command Semete resumes his posture.

Ukete with his right fist at his right hip utters the kiai and strikes at Semete's middle body with his left fist (*fig.* 94).

Fig. 93

(3) At the word of command Semete draws back his left foot to the preparatory posture.

Ukete advances his left foot to the preparatory posture. Semete and Ukete then exchange roles and repeat the practice.

At the end of the demonstration Semete and Ukete face each other at a distance of about three feet and after saluting in the prescribed manner, turn to the shrine and the Master in charge of the demonstration and repeat the salutation.

Zealous practice of these *Yakusoku Kumite* will enable you to understand the meaning and purpose of all the kumites. The kumite kata are of course designed to train you to move your body so as to be ready for a genuine emergency in which your life might be threatened. The four following precepts should, therefore, be borne in mind: (1) Since the Kumite Kata are intended to apply to real conditions you should study them in that spirit. (2) If you treat them in a frivolous mood you will run the risk of injury. (3) When you attack your opponent do so with the utmost intensity of purpose, in other words, without actually striking, do not pull punches. You must remain unperturbed if your opponent beats off your attack, concentrate your strength and when it is your turn to act as defender, then however powerful the attack, you should meet it fully confident in your ability to ward it off. (4) The *Ten-no-Kata* just described are practised as two movements of defence and attack in each case but as you become more proficient you should practise them as a single movement. At the instant of defence your counter-attack should already be delivered, the two actions must appear to the eye to be merged into one.

In addition to the Yakusoku Kumite, karate recognizes three other classes of kumite from which the following brief examples must suffice:

TANSHIKI KUMITE KATA (Simple Kumite Kata): (1) 'A' aims a blow at 'B's' face with his right fist. 'B' steps a pace to the rear with his right foot and as he does so his left fist, moving strongly downwards from above, blocks 'A's' right forearm and he simultaneously strikes at 'B's' middle body with his right fist. As this defence is executed from the inside it is known as the inner-defence, or uchi-uke. (2) 'A' aims a blow at 'B's' face with his right fist. 'B' steps back with his left foot and holds his right fist in the jodan-uke, or upper level defence, and simultaneously strikes at 'A's' armpit with his left fist. As this defence is executed from the direction of 'A's' outer body it is known as the outer-defence, or soto-uke. 'A' in his turn attacks with his left fist, and 'B' steps back on his right leg and effects an outer defence with his left fist. The relationship between hand and leg corresponds respectively to that between the middle level defence (chudan-uke) and the lower level defence (gedan-uke). It is imperative that all these movements should be practised by both partners, with exchange of roles, until mastery of them has been achieved.

FUKUSHIKI KUMITE KATA (Double Kumite Kata). 'A' attacks 'B' and 'B' defends himself and counter-attacks. 'A' in his turn wards off this attack and again attacks 'B'. In this way attack, defence and counter-attack are repeated several times until, eventually, action and reaction become almost reflex. There are variations of this kumite involving more complicated and difficult movements. JIYU KUMITE (Free or Contest Kumite). In this kumite the partners freely apply both defensive and offensive techniques as though engaged in actual combat. The greatest care must be taken to halt the blow or kick before it actually touches the partner, otherwise there would be a grave risk of serious injury. For this reason it is not advisable for novices to engage in Jiyu Kumite Kata until their teachers are satisfied that they have acquired a sufficient degree of skill and control. And under no circumstances should they be practised outside of a recognised Karate Club or without supervision by a master.